Meet the shark

The shark is one of the fastest fish in the sea. Every part of its body is perfect for the water – its light, bendy skeleton, its smooth, sleek shape and its powerful fins and tail. These make many sharks into deadly hunters. But not all sharks are fast and fierce. Some, such as the whale shark, are gentle giants that feed only on the tiniest creatures in the sea.

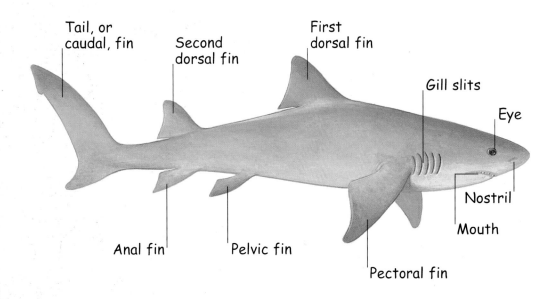

Tail, or caudal, fin

Second dorsal fin

First dorsal fin

Gill slits

Eye

Nostril

Mouth

Anal fin

Pelvic fin

Pectoral fin

A shark's body
Most fish have skeletons made of hard bone, but a shark's skeleton is made of light, flexible cartilage. This allows the shark to twist and turn very quickly. Like all fish, sharks use their gills to take in oxygen from the water.

Grey reef shark hunting for prey over a coral reef

4

My Best Book of
Sharks

Claire Llewellyn

KING*f*ISHER

Contents

Author: Claire Llewellyn
Consultant: Brian Harris, London
   Zoo Aquarium
Senior editor: Sarah Milan
Editor: Sue Nicholson
Designer: Malcolm Parchment
Production controller: Caroline Jackson
Illustrators: Ray Grinaway,
   Roger Stewart

KINGFISHER
Kingfisher Publications Plc,
New Penderel House,
283–288 High Holborn,
London WC1V 7HZ
www.kingfisherpub.com

First published by Kingfisher
Publications Plc 1999

First published in paperback 2001

10 9 8 7 6 5 4 3 2 (HB)
1TR/0399/WKT/MAR(MAR)/128/KMA
10 9 8 7 6 5 4 3 2 1 (PB)
BS+JKT/0802/WKT/MA/115TPMA

Copyright © Kingfisher
Publications Plc 1999

A CIP catalogue record for this book
is available from the British Library.

ISBN 0 7534 0304 8 (HB)
ISBN 0 7534 0561 X (PB)

Printed in Hong Kong

A world of sharks

There are about 375 kinds of shark, and they come in all sorts of colours, shapes and sizes. Many sharks are sleek and slim. Others are flabby and flat. Some are silver-grey. Others are brown, blue, spotty or striped. Many sharks are darker on top and paler underneath. This is called countershading. It makes a shark much harder to spot – both from below, when it is seen against the light, and from above, against the murky sea.

Pygmy shark
(20cm long)

Cookiecutter shark
(50cm long)

Dogfish shark
(40-60cm long)

Tasselled wobbegon shark (1.25m long)

Sawshark
(1.4m long)

Port Jackson shark
(1.5m long)

Frilled shark
(1.96m long)

Leopard shark
(1.8m long)

Blue shark
(3.2m long)

Angelshark
(1.25m long)

Lemon shark
(3.4m long)

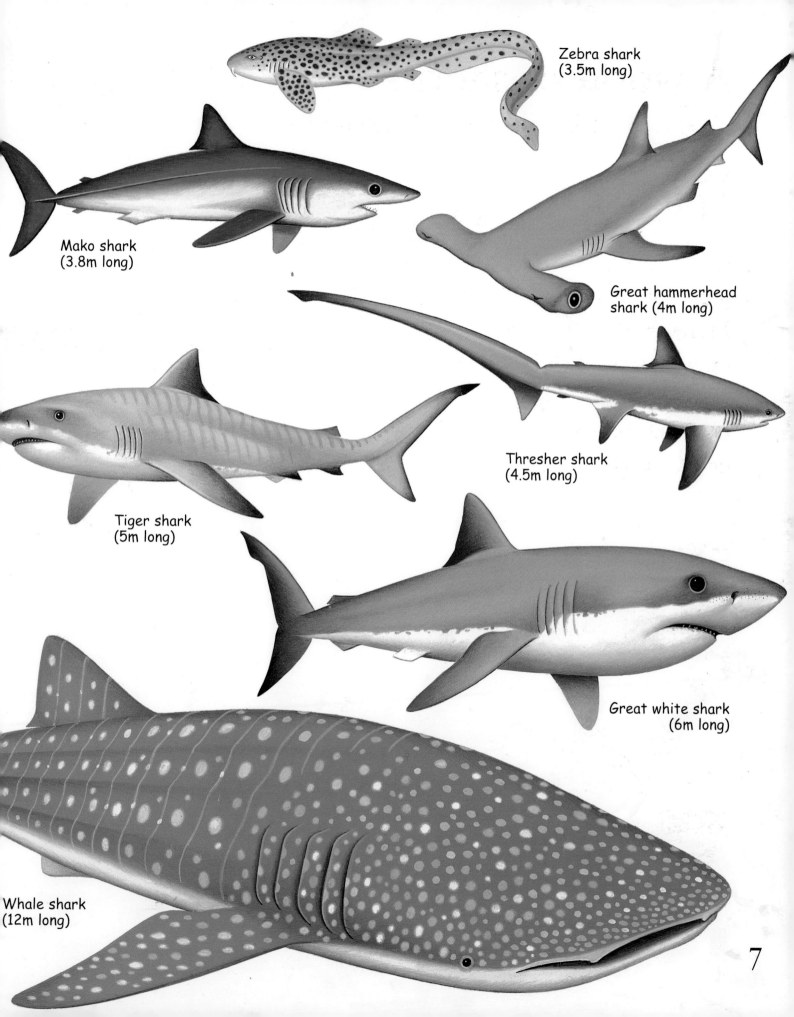

Zebra shark
(3.5m long)

Mako shark
(3.8m long)

Great hammerhead
shark (4m long)

Thresher shark
(4.5m long)

Tiger shark
(5m long)

Great white shark
(6m long)

Whale shark
(12m long)

7

Swimming champions

A shark hardly seems to move as it swims along. It simply flicks its tail from side to side to push its body through the water. It uses its fins to turn, stop, rise or dive. Most fish have soft, bendy fins that can be stretched out or tucked back. But a shark's fins are stiff and stick out like paddles, and cannot be folded away.

Grey smooth-hound sharks swimming along the seabed

Shark skin
Most sharks' skin is covered with tiny, thorny teeth called denticles. If you stroked the skin from back to front, it could cut your hand.

Shark tails

Shark tails come in different shapes. Bull and thresher sharks have long, streamlined tails that slice through the water so the sharks can quickly twist and turn. The swell shark's broader tail gently wafts the water so that the fish can cruise along the seabed. The balanced shape of the great white's tail allows it – and others like it – to swim the fastest of all.

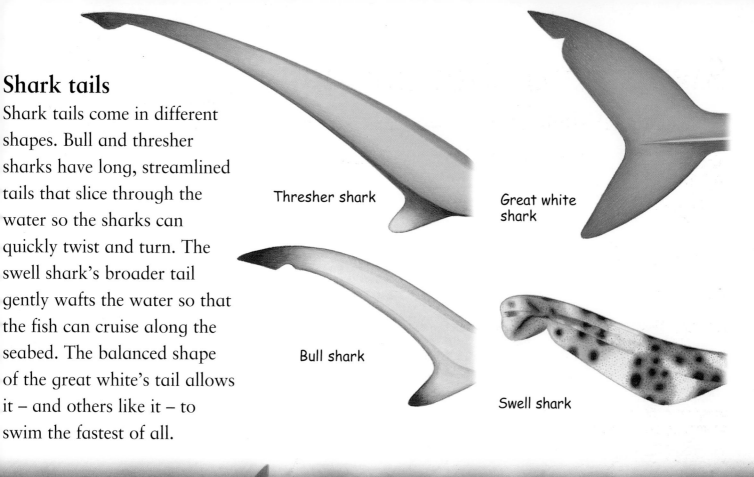

Thresher shark

Great white shark

Bull shark

Swell shark

Baby sharks

Baby sharks are known as pups, and they grow in different ways. Most grow from eggs in their mother's body, and are born into the sea. Others grow from eggs that are laid in water. Each egg sits in its own little case, which hardens to protect the growing pup. The shark hatches out when it is fully grown, and swims off to hide somewhere safe. Now it must look after itself – its mother leaves it quite alone.

Hammerhead shark pups

Born into the sea

Shark pups slip out through an opening in their mother's body. They are joined to their mother by tiny cords, which break as the pups swim away.

Lemon shark pups

Cat shark
eggcase and pup

Horn shark
eggcase and pup

Dogfish
shark eggcases
(also called
mermaid's
purses)

Shark eggcases

Eggcases are tough and
built to last. A cat shark's
eggcases have tiny tendrils
that cling tightly to plants.

A horn shark's eggcases
survive in cracks in the
rocks. Other eggcases settle
on the seabed. Many get
eaten before the pups hatch.

Tendrils of
cat shark's
eggcase wraps
around plant

Dogfish shark pup
(10cm long)

Yolk
sac

Dogfish shark
ready to hatch

Dogfish shark eggs

Dogfish sharks lay about 20 eggs, often in a
clump of seaweed. Each egg contains a sac
of yolk for the pup to feed on as it grows.
The eggs take nine months to hatch. The
pups look just like their parents, but smaller.

11

Homing in

Sharks are skilful at finding their prey in the vast, dark world of the ocean. They feel movements in the water from far away. They can smell the faintest whiff of blood. They can even pick up the electrical signals from an animal's beating heart. Most sharks choose to hunt alone, but sometimes a group will attack the same prey. The sharks snap wildly and even bite one another in a savage feeding frenzy.

Eye

Nostril

Hammerhead hunter

A hammerhead shark has an eye and a nostril on each end of its hammer-shaped head. As it swims along, it swings its head from one side to another, picking up signals from the water.

Grey reef sharks attack a tuna fish in a feeding frenzy

The deadly jaws

Sharks feed on nearly every creature in the sea. They catch penguins, seals, turtles, fish and crabs. Because different kinds of shark feed on different kinds of food, they have different-shaped jaws and teeth. A few teeth drop out during every meal, but new ones move up to take their place. A shark goes through hundreds of teeth during its lifetime.

Shaken to bits

Sharks cannot chew. If a meal is too large to swallow whole, they shake it from side to side to saw it into chunks.

Ragged teeth

The sandtiger shark (also known as the ragged tooth or grey nurse shark) has several rows of sharp, spiky teeth. Each tooth is about 4cm long.

Types of teeth

A shark's teeth are a tool kit to catch and cut up its food. Long, spiky teeth can skewer a slithery octopus or squid. Serrated teeth can saw through bony fish. Hard, flat teeth can grind up shellfish, such as lobsters and crabs, and even crunch through a tough turtle shell.

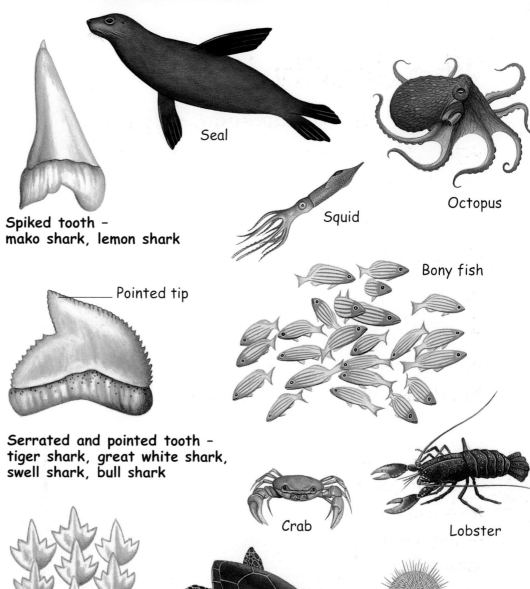

Seal

Octopus

Squid

Bony fish

**Spiked tooth –
mako shark, lemon shark**

Pointed tip

**Serrated and pointed tooth –
tiger shark, great white shark,
swell shark, bull shark**

**Grinding teeth –
Port Jackson shark,
nurse shark**

Crab

Lobster

Sea
urchin

Turtle

**Sandtiger shark
(3m long)**

**Cookiecutter
shark**

Lips form a round
cup that sucks
hold of prey

A cookiecutter bite

A cookiecutter shark's jaws are perfectly round, like a cookie, or biscuit, cutter. When it sinks its teeth into a seal or whale, it tears out a cookie-shaped mouthful.

15

Gentle giants

The whale shark is the world's biggest fish, yet it feeds on minuscule creatures. As the shark cruises along near the surface of the ocean, it sucks in great mouthfuls of water. This pours through curtains of long, fine bristles that hang inside the shark's mouth. The bristles work like filters or a sieve, trapping shoals of plankton and schools of tiny fish, which the shark then swallows.

Whale shark teeth

Tiny teeth
Whale and basking sharks have tiny teeth, about half the size of your little fingernail. They do not use them to bite or crush their food, but to help them spit it out now and again.

Basking sharks

Basking sharks swim along with their mouth wide open, trapping tiny sea creatures, such as shrimps and plankton.

Plankton

Plankton is the name given to the tiny creatures that drift in the sea. You can only see them under a microscope.

Sharks on the seabed

Some sharks hide at the bottom of the sea to rest or pounce on their prey. Their flat bodies, brown skin and blotchy markings help them blend in with the stones or sand. One shark, the tasselled wobbegong, has frills of skin around its mouth. These look so much like bits of seaweed that small fish swim up to nibble them and end up being eaten themselves.

Having a rest
Port Jackson sharks like to feed at night. They spend the day resting in sandy caves or in gaps between the rocks.

The tasselled wobbegong shark waiting for its next meal

Angel in the sand

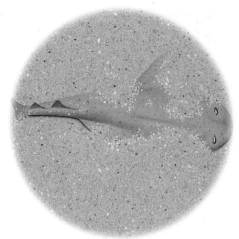

1 The angelshark spends much of its life resting and feeding on the seabed.

2 It flaps its fins to cover itself with sand. It is now almost invisible.

3 Its two eyes lie on the top of its head so that it can still keep a look-out for food.

Luminous sharks

A few sharks that live in deep, dark water have special ways of using light. The massive mouth of a megamouth shark shines with a silvery glow. This may attract the tasty shoals of plankton that megamouths like to eat. The cookiecutter shark also uses light. Its belly glows a luminous green. This may attract a nearby animal, such as a whale, that is large enough to bite.

Bright lanterns

Lantern sharks swim in large shoals. Each fish is covered with luminous slime that glows in the dark. Scientists believe that this glowing slime may help the fish keep their place in the shoal.

Megamouth sharks live in such deep water that only six or so have ever been found

Shark attack!

Some sharks can be dangerous to humans. About 30 kinds of shark, including the bull shark, tiger shark and great white shark, have attacked people in the water. Some have even overturned sailing boats. Large, meat-eating sharks have powerful jaws, and when they attack they often kill. However, shark attacks are very rare. There are only about 100 every year. You are much more likely to be struck by lightning than be attacked by a shark.

DO: Tuck up legs and keep as still and quiet as possible

DON'T: Shout, splash and kick legs in the water

Seal or surfer?

Sharks don't seem to like the taste of people. Usually, they do not eat people they attack.

Perhaps they bite swimmers by mistake – after all, from under the water, a surfer looks just like a seal.

Safety at sea

If someone falls overboard into the sea, they should not shout, splash or kick their legs in the water. Sharks are attracted to noise and movement, and may mistake a splashing person for a shoal of fish.

Sea drama
Sound travels a long way under water. The noise of people splashing in the sea and the whirr of a rescue helicopter's rotor blades may attract sharks from several kilometres away.

Sharks in danger

Every year, about 100 million sharks are killed. Most of them are killed for their skin, meat and fins. Some are killed for sport. Others are killed by accident when they swim into fishing nets or shark nets. Some kinds of shark take years to have young, and may have just one pup a year. If more sharks die than are born each year, they will become extinct.

Made from sharks

Sharks are killed to make creams, cures for illnesses and shark fin soup. Most of these goods can be made in other ways. The others we could live without.

Death trap

Harmless sharks are sometimes killed in nets put up to protect swimmers from more dangerous sharks.

Shark fin soup is popular in many countries in Asia.

Capsules of shark liver oil

Skin cream

Lipstick

A shark-tooth necklace is believed to give the wearer strength.

A sporting chance?

Some fast-swimming sharks, such as the mako shark, are the "big game" of the sea. In the past, many were killed for sport. Today, anglers are encouraged to release them instead.

25

Studying sharks

Scientists still have many questions about sharks. How long do they live? How fast do they grow? How far do they swim? To help find the answers, scientists clip sonic tags to sharks' fins. The tags give out signals that the scientists can follow. Over the years, scientists have studied thousands of sharks, and are learning more about them. And the more they know, the better chance they have of saving them from extinction.

Spear

Label asking where the shark was caught, its length and weight

Metal-tipped dart tag

Shark tags

Scientists use long spears to tag sharks in the water. A tag's label asks any angler who catches the shark to send in information about it.

Shark speedometer

Sometimes a tiny propeller is tied to a shark's dorsal fin. The propeller measures how fast the shark moves as it cruises through the sea.

Tagging a shark
Tagging is harmless to
sharks as long as it is done
quickly. In the long run, it
may help to protect them
from extinction.

Shark gear

Many divers like to swim with sharks. They must protect themselves in case they are attacked. Most divers wear special suits made of metal mesh. Some swim inside plastic scooters. To watch or photograph more dangerous sharks, divers stay inside a metal cage. They tie a bag of bait to the bars of the cage – then all they have to do is wait!

Bag of fish to act as bait

Steel cage

Shark scooter

Motor

Scary but safe

Sharks are attracted by metal, but a steel cage won't break even if it is torpedoed by a great white shark.

Plastic scooter

This shark scooter is made of strong, clear plastic. The divers can see well and move around freely.

28

Mask

Chainmail hood

Close-up of Neptunic's steel rings

Underwater armour

In the water, divers wear a heavy metal suit called a neptunic. The neptunic is made of about 400,000 tiny stainless steel rings, which link together to form a fine chainmail. The rings stop a shark's teeth from piercing the skin but won't prevent a nasty bruise.

Aqualung containing air for the diver to breathe

Chainmail gloves

Wet suit

Flippers

Underwater camera ar light

Neptunic diving suit

29

Seeing sharks

You don't have to get wet to see a shark! You can watch one at an aquarium through a wall of glass. Why not sketch, make notes about, or photograph the different kinds of shark you see? Of course, an aquarium is too small for large, fast sharks. These fish need a lot of space and are much better off in the open sea.

Making a shark factfile, with notes, photographs and sketches

An all-round view

Some aquariums have ocean tanks big enough to house a whole coral reef. As visitors walk through tunnels of glass, they enjoy an amazing view of different kinds of shark, such as smooth-hounds, sand tigers or white tip reef sharks.

Glossary

aqualung A container of air that divers carry on their back so that they can breathe under the water.

cartilage The rubbery or gristly material that forms a shark's skeleton.

coral reef A long line of coral that lies below the water in warm, shallow parts of the sea. Coral is built by tiny animals.

countershading The name given to the shading on sharks and many other fish. The darker back and paler belly makes them harder to see, either from above looking down into deep, dark water, or from below, looking up towards bright sunlight.

denticles The small, stiff, thorny scales that make up a shark's rough skin.

extinct No longer living on Earth. An animal becomes extinct when not one of its kind is alive.

feeding frenzy The activity that takes place among feeding sharks. They become excited, biting at anything close by.

fish An animal with a backbone that lives in water and breathes through gills. There are about 24,620 known kinds of fish. Some live in freshwater; some in saltwater. Some, such as the bull shark, can live in both.

gill The part of a fish's body that allows it to breathe under water. The gills soak up oxygen that has dissolved in the water. On most fish, the gills are covered with flaps of skin. On sharks, they are slits.

luminous Giving out a bright light.

neptunic A diving suit made of thousands of small steel rings. Divers wear a neptunic to protect themselves from sharks.

oxygen A gas that all animals need to breathe in order to survive. Oxygen is one of the gases found in the air. It is also found in water.

plankton Microscopic plants and animals that live in the sea.

predator A hunter.

prey An animal hunted by another for food.

pup A baby shark.

serrated Having a sharp, zigzag edge like a saw or steak knife.

shellfish A sea creature with a hard, protective shell, such as a crab or lobster.

skeleton The frame inside an animal's body that protects it and holds it up. Most fish have a bony skeleton, but a shark's skeleton is made of tough, bendy cartilage, like the stuff at the end of your nose.

streamlined Having a smooth body shape that moves easily through the water.

Index

Blueberry Girl

written by Neil Gaiman

illustrated by Charles Vess

BLOOMSBURY

LONDON BERLIN NEW YORK

Ladies
of
light
and
ladies
of
darkness
and
ladies
of
never-
you-
mind,

this is a prayer for a blueberry girl.

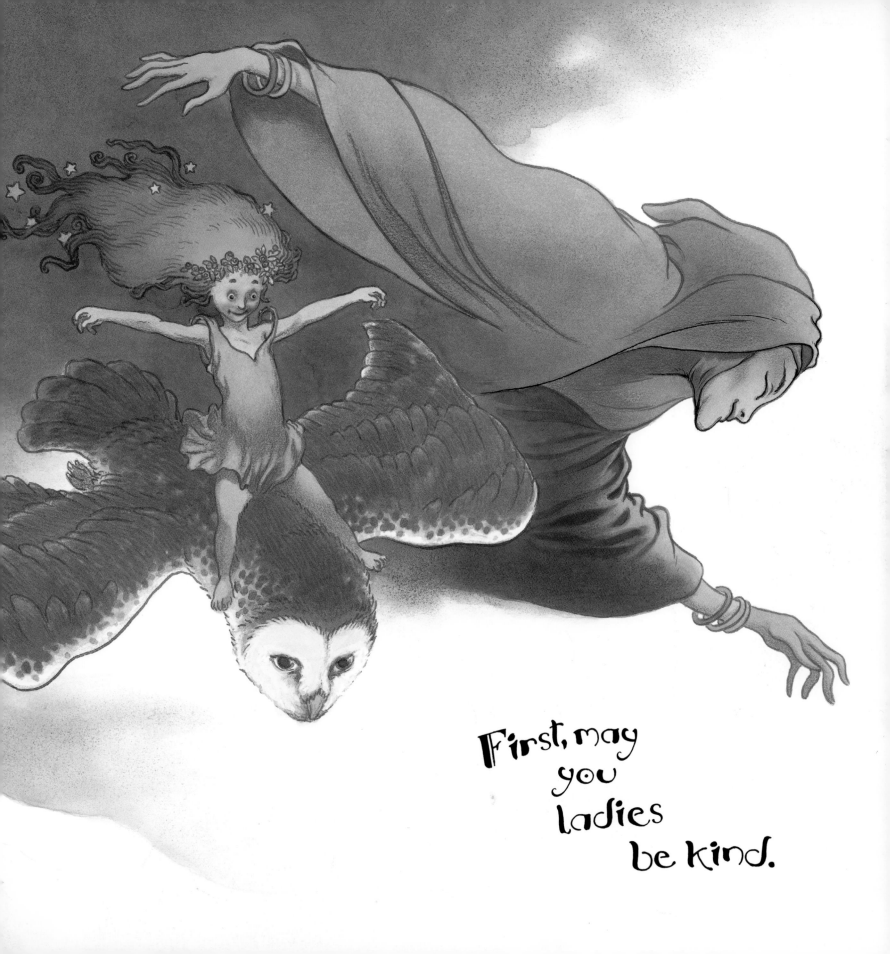

First, may
you
ladies
be kind.

Keep her from spindles and sleeps at sixteen,

let her stay waking and wise.

Nightmares at three or bad husbands at thirty,

These will not trouble her eyes.

Dull days at forty,
   false friends at fifteen –
let her have
      brave days
         and
            truth,

Let her go places
that we've never been,
trust and
delight
in
her
youth.

Ladies of grace and ladies of favour

and

ladies of merciful night,

this is a prayer
for a blueberry girl.

Grant
her your
clearness
of
sight.

Words
can
be
worrisome,
people
complex,

motives
and
manners
unclear,

Grant her the wisdom to choose
her path right,

free from
unkindness
and fear.

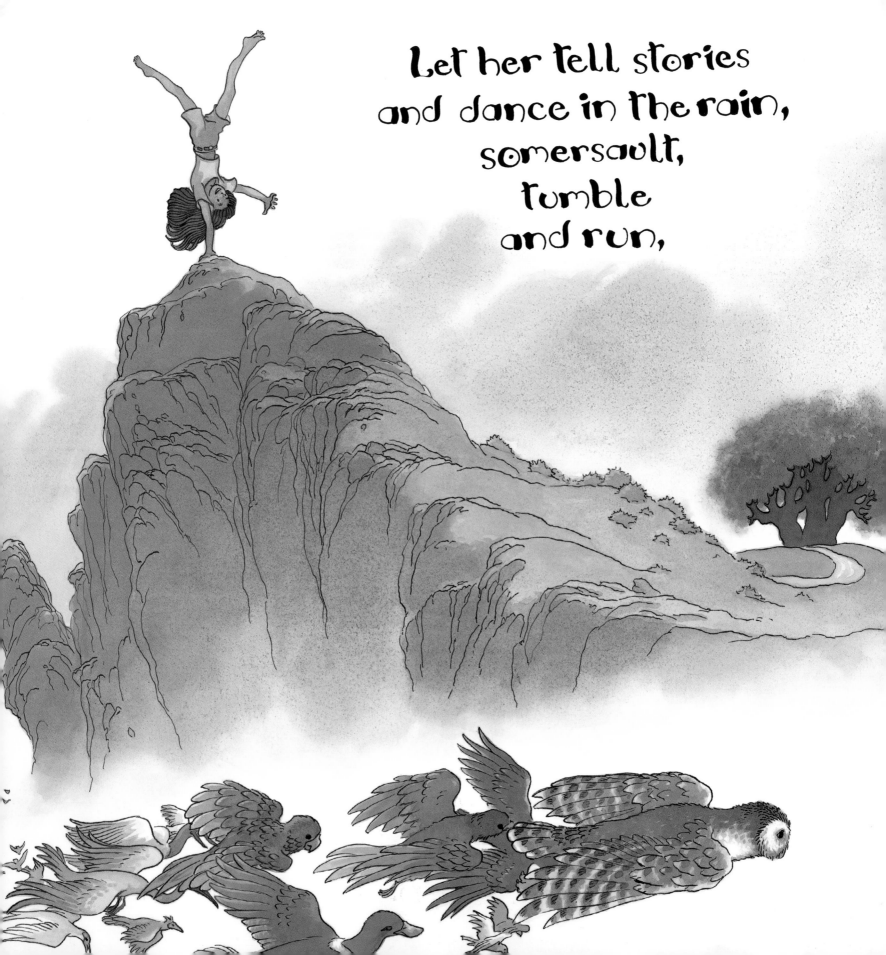

Let her tell stories
and dance in the rain,
somersault,
tumble
and run,

her
joys
must
be high
as her
sorrows
are
deep.

Let her grow
like a weed in
the sun.

Ladies
of
paradox,
ladies
of
measure,
ladies
of
shadows
that
fall,

this is a prayer
for a blueberry girl.

Words written clear on a wall.

Help her to help
herself,
help her to
stand,

help her
to lose
and
to find.

Teach
her
we're
only
as
big as our
dreams.

Show her that fortune is blind.

Truth is a thing she must find for herself, precious and rare as a pearl.

Give
her
all
these
and a
little
bit
more...

Gifts for a blueberry girl.

I wrote this for Tori, and for
Tash, when she was only a bump
and a due date. With love, Neil

This one is for MY MOM, who was
always there for me, MY first
admirer and critic. All MY love
from your son, Charles

Bloomsbury Publishing, London, Berlin and New York

First published in Great Britain in March 2009 by Bloomsbury Publishing Plc
36 Soho Square, London, WID 3QY

This paperback edition first published in 2010

First published in the U.S. in 2009 by HarperCollins Children's Books
a division of HarperCollins Publishers, 1350 Avenue of the Americas, New York, NY 10C

Published by arrangement with HarperCollins Children's Books,
a division of HarperCollins Publishers

Text copyright © Neil Gaiman 2009
Illustrations copyright © Charles Vess 2009
The moral rights of the author and illustrator have been asserted

A CIP catalogue record of this book is available from the British Library

ISBN 978 0 7475 9598 4

Typography by Charles Vess

Printed in China by C&C Offset Printing Co Ltd, Shenzhen, Guangdong

1 3 5 7 9 10 8 6 4 2

All papers used by Bloomsbury Publishing are natural, recyclable products
made from wood grown in well-managed forests. The manufacturing processes
conform to the environmental regulations of the country of origin

www.bloomsbury.com/childrens
www.neilgaiman.com
www.greenmanpress.com